Pronouns

Them!

You!

It!

written by Ann Heinrichs

illustrated by Dan McGeehan and David Moore

The Child's World

Published by The Child's World®
1980 Lookout Drive • Mankato, MN 56003-1705
800-599-READ • www.childsworld.com

ACKNOWLEDGMENTS
The Child's World®: Mary Berendes, Publishing Director
The Design Lab: Design and page production
Red Line Editorial: Editorial direction

LIBRARY OF CONGRESS CATALOGING-IN-PUBLICATION DATA
Heinrichs, Ann.
  Pronouns / by Ann Heinrichs ; illustrated by Dan McGeehan and David
Moore.
    p. cm.
  Includes bibliographical references and index.
  ISBN 978-1-60253-432-2 (library bound : alk. paper)
  1. English language—Pronoun—Juvenile literature. I. McGeehan, Dan,
ill. II. Moore, David, ill. III. Title.
  PE1261.H373 2010
  428.2—dc22   2010011461

Printed in the United States of America in Mankato, Minnesota.
July 2010
F11538

ABOUT THE AUTHOR

Ann Heinrichs was lucky. Every year from
grade three through grade eight, she had a
big, fat grammar textbook and a grammar
workbook. She feels that this prepared her
for life. She is now the author of more than
100 books for children and young adults.
She has also enjoyed successful careers as
a children's book editor and an advertising
copywriter. Ann grew up in Fort Smith,
Arkansas, and lives in Chicago, Illinois.

ABOUT THE ILLUSTRATORS

Dan McGeehan spent his younger years
as an actor, author, playwright, cartoonist,
editor, and even as a casket maker. Now he
spends his days drawing little monsters!

David Moore is an illustration instructor
at a university who loves painting and
flying airplanes. Watching his youngest
daughter draw inspires David to illustrate
children's books.

You!

TABLE OF CONTENTS

What Is a Pronoun?

Matthew threw the stick and waited. The dogs ran after the stick, but the dogs couldn't find the stick. Matthew was sure Matthew had thrown the stick near the dogs.

Whew! That's a lot of words! Now try this:

Matthew threw the stick and waited. The dogs ran after it, but they couldn't find it. He was sure he had thrown it near them.

Isn't that easier? That's because we used **pronouns**. It, they, them, and he took the place of *the stick*, *the dogs*, and *Matthew*. Pronouns stand in for other **nouns**. Pronouns usually refer to people or things.

I'm throwing it to you!

One or More?

Some pronouns refer to just one person or thing. These pronouns are **singular**. Some singular pronouns are I, me, he, him, she, her, and it.

Jack ran through the field.
He ran through it.

Some pronouns refer to two or more things. These pronouns are **plural**. Some plural pronouns are we, us, they, and them.

The birds fought over the worms.
They fought over them.

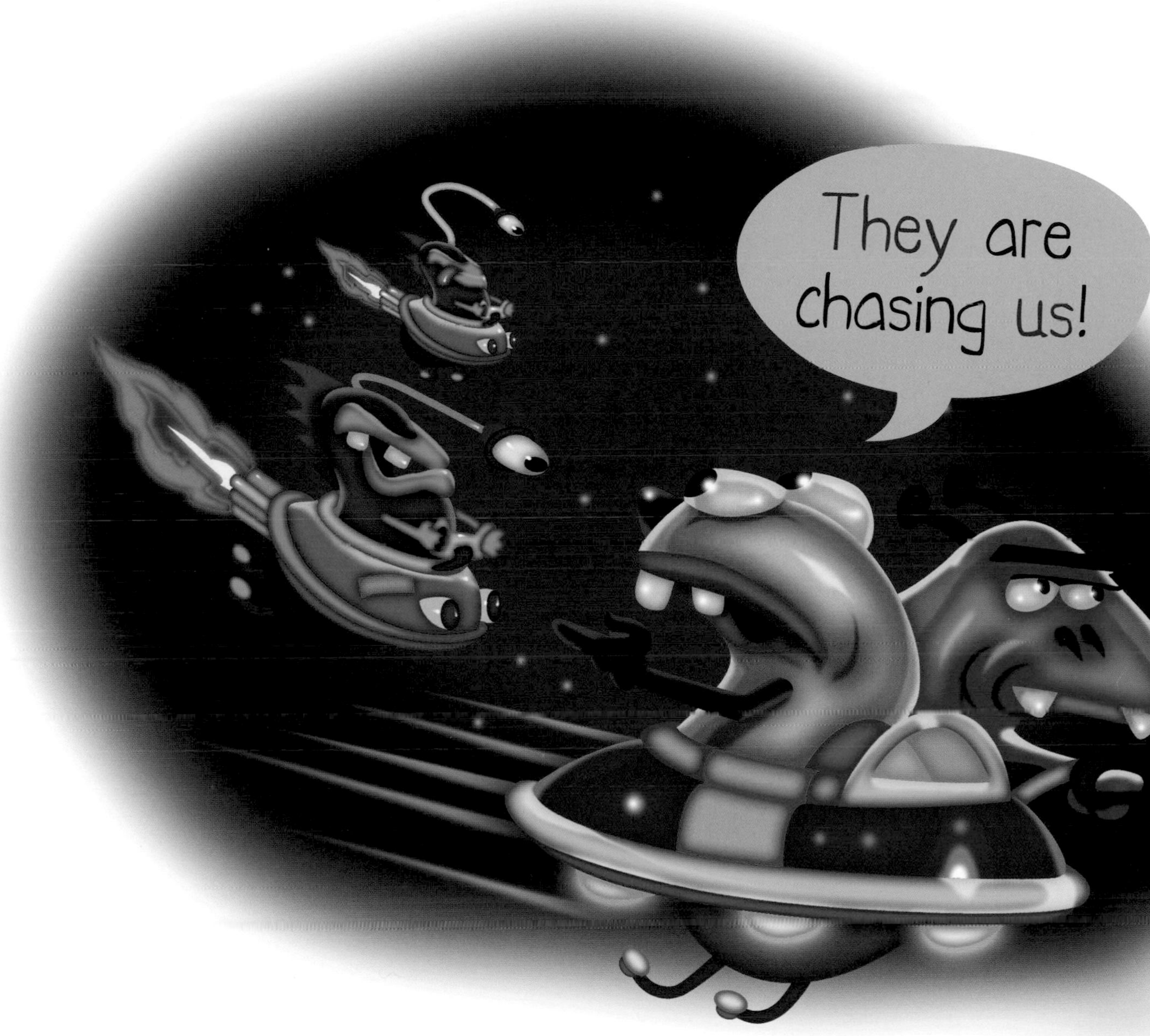
They are chasing us!

The Special Case of You

"How are you doing?"

"I'm fine. What did you do this weekend?"

In this conversation, you is singular. Each friend is talking to just one person.

"What are you all doing after school?"

In this case, you is plural. It refers to a group of people.

I Grabbed It!

Some pronouns refer to the person or thing taking action in a sentence.

I grabbed the ball.

He landed the spaceship.

It bit the apple!

The pronouns taking action are I, he, and it.

11

It Grabbed Me!

Other pronouns refer to the thing receiving the action.

Kevin gave the cat to them.

The monster grabbed me.

The dog caught it.

The pronouns receiving the action are them, me, and it.

Choosing the right pronoun depends on who is taking or receiving the action.

They saw her.

Then she saw them.

The fish is grabbing me.

Using the wrong pronoun sounds strange!
You wouldn't say, "The puppy jumped on she."
You'd say, "The puppy jumped on her."

You wouldn't say, "Us saw an airplane." You'd say,
"We saw an airplane."

I like the monster. The monster likes me.

You and it work both ways.

It likes to eat. The cat likes it.

You answered the question.
The teacher called on you.

Doing the action	Happening to
I	me
you	you
he, she, it	him, her, it
we	us
they	them

I'll Keep It to Myself

Consider these sentences:

> She patted me on the back.
>
> I patted myself on the back.

Why switch to myself in the second sentence? In the second case, the person patting and getting patted are the same. We use special pronouns to show that a person is both doing and receiving an action: myself, yourself, himself, herself, itself, ourselves, themselves, and yourselves.

Yours or Mine?

Give me back that ball! It's mine!

Take this book. It's yours.

Josh has his pen, and Emily has hers.

This popcorn belongs to the twins.
These apples are theirs, too.

Mine, yours, his, hers, and theirs show who owns the ball, book, pens, and snacks. Can you name the owners?

Me goes with mine.
You goes with yours.
Josh goes with his.
Emily goes with hers.
The twins go with theirs.

This hat is mine.
You have yours.

19

This, That, These, or Those?

Imagine pointing your finger at some pies and saying,

"This is apple, and that is pumpkin."

The apple pie is closer to you, isn't it? How did you know? This shows things nearby, while that points to things farther away. What if there was more than one pie?

"These are strawberry, and those are pecan."

In that case, those shows that the pecan pies are farther away.

Something, Nothing

Nicole said something, and everybody laughed.

What did Nicole say? Who laughed? We don't know for sure. You can use pronouns when you don't know exactly what happened or who did it.

Some more of these pronouns are: anyone, any, somebody, nothing, every, several, most, none.

There is nobody here!

How to Learn More

AT THE LIBRARY

Cleary, Brian P. *I and You and Don't Forget Who: What Is a Pronoun?*
Minneapolis, MN: First Avenue Editions, 2006.

Fisher, Doris. *Slam Dunk Pronouns*. Pleasantville, NY: Gareth Stevens, 2008.

Heller, Ruth. *Mine, All Mine: A Book about Pronouns*. New York: Puffin
Books, 1999.

Martin, Justin McCory. *The Planet Without Pronouns.* New York: Scholastic,
2004.

McClarnon, Marciann. *Painless Junior Grammar*. Hauppauge, NY: Barron's
Educational Series, 2007.

Schoolhouse Rock: Grammar Classroom Edition. Dir. Tom Warburton.
Interactive DVD. Walt Disney, 2007.

ON THE WEB

Visit our home page for lots of links about grammar: *childsworld.com/links*

NOTE TO PARENTS, TEACHERS AND LIBRARIANS: We routinely check our Web links to make sure they're
safe, active sites—so encourage your readers to check them out!

Glossary

nouns (NOUNS): Words that name people, places, and things. *Claire*, *Connecticut*, and *cookie* are nouns.

plural (PLOOR-uhl): A word is plural if it names more than one thing. *We* and *they* are plural pronouns.

pronouns (PROH-nouns): Words that stand in for other nouns. *I*, *he*, *it*, and *them* are pronouns.

singular (SING-gyu-lur): A word is singular if it names one thing. *I* and *she* are singular pronouns.

24

Index